T0096231

RECLAIMING HUMANITY

RECLAIMING HUMANITY

A GUIDE
TO MAINTAINING THE INNER WORLD
OF THE CHILD FACING ONGOING TRAUMA

Norman J. Fried PhD

URIM PUBLICATIONS
Jerusalem • New York

Reclaiming Humanity: A Guide to Maintaining
the Inner World of the Child facing Ongoing Trauma

by Norman J. Fried

Copyright © 2017 Norman J. Fried

Typeset by Ariel Walden

Printed in Israel

First Edition

ISBN 978-965-524-212-6

Urim Publications, P.O. Box 52287
Jerusalem 9152102 Israel

www.UrimPublications.com

Library of Congress Cataloging-in-Publication Data

Names: Fried, Norman J., author.
Title: Reclaiming humanity : a guide to maintaining the inner
    world of the child facing ongoing trauma / Norman J. Fried,
    PhD.
Description: Jerusalem ; New York : Urim Publications, [2017]
Identifiers: LCCN 2017039019 | ISBN 9789655242126
    (hardback)
Subjects: LCSH: Psychic trauma in children—Treatment. | Child
    mental health. | BISAC: PSYCHOLOGY / Psychotherapy /
    Child & Adolescent. | PSYCHOLOGY / Social Psychology. |
    RELIGION / Judaism / General.
Classification: LCC RJ506.P66 F75 2017 | DDC 618.928521—
    dc23 LC record available at https://lccn.loc.gov/2017039019

To live is to build a ship and a harbor
at the same time. And to finish the harbor
long after the ship has gone down.

Yehuda Amichai

For Scott Fried

My brother and mentor

Contents

Introduction

THE INNER WORLD of the healthy child is filled with
wonder, awe and faith in the benevolence of a fair and just
world. But for children growing up in many countries and
cultures around the world, where security, safety and the
promise of peace are challenged, if not entirely broken,
a belief in the benevolence of the world and its people is
often too hard to achieve. The children in war-torn areas
live constantly from protective shield to protective shield,
and cease fire to cease fire. Many of these children are neg-
atively impacted by sudden and intrusive alerts; or by the
reality of the trauma of having a loved one on the front
line – a father or older brother or sister. In some cases,
both the parent and the sibling are in combat. Eventually,
a new methodology or internal philosophy is born. For the
child, it is a methodology of fear and destruction. Hamas,
like the serpent in the center of the Garden of Eden, comes
up from beneath the tunnels and challenges Israel's ethical
norm. Supporters of ISIS attack public gatherings in Paris,
and related terrorist factions kill innocent victims in San
Bernardino, California; Dallas, Texas; and Orlando, Flor-
ida, to name only a few. Through fear and trauma, terrorism incites the civilian to rebellion and war. As a result, the

promise of a covenant fulfilled becomes weakened. Like the serpent who said to Adam:

> For God knows that on the day that you eat of it, then your eyes shall be opened, and you shall be as gods, knowing good and evil,

So too does violence challenge our faith in the fulfillment of God's word. We discover that evil subsists alongside good; and that the waves of chaos all too often crash down on the shores of safety and order. Contemporary man, like Adam, must fight against this chaos or he is bound to become a victim of the same trap created by the serpent before him.

This dialectic has been the central theme of the historical narrative of the Jewish people. As Rabbi Joseph Soloveitchik, known by his students as the Rav, asserts, Jewish history is filled with the unending swing of the ethical pendulum. At times, we see this in the dialectical form of people, at other times in the form of events. For example, Adam's conflict with the serpent is later followed by Cain's struggle with Abel, Noah's discord with his generation of sinners, Isaac's relationship with Ishmael, Jacob and his nemesis Esau, the elevation of Jacob's family in Egypt with the generations of Jewish slavery that followed, and Moses' ultimate confrontation with Pharaoh. As the pendulum swings, an ethical personality or event collides with a chaotic one, and the fate of the Jewish people is left hanging in the balance.

Who will win this time? How can parent and child, facing ongoing trauma in a world filled with evil and chaos, reclaim an ethical norm and maintain a sense of humanity?

The answer may be found in Jewish history itself, for in the Torah we see how human tension is often settled through the connection of man to a healthy other; a belief in a higher being, or a re-connection with God and the covenant itself. Through this connection, man's moral imperative becomes re-awakened, and he becomes more aware of his innate ethical drive. A Jewish ethical life through a connection with God impels us to reconcile chaos with harmony.

We see the healing power of this connection throughout the Torah. Biblical man has always wrestled with chaos, suffering and despair before being blessed with a more cathartic, pure and noble state of mind. The binding of Isaac and the paradoxical expression of God's love; Jacob's struggle with the angel and his experience of a daybreak filled with promise and hope; the Israelites' arduous journey through the desert and their ultimate arrival to the Promised Land; the deaths of Nadab and Abihu and man's acknowledgement to live life to its fullest measure; Jonah, alone in the belly of darkness and his discovery of faith; and Job in his fatal tempest who learned of his promise of redemption in the World to Come, are all examples of the healing power of the covenant.

Perhaps the greatest example of the redemptive power of connection is that of Moses and God. As the Rav asserts, man, through Moses, became a *shaliach*, a messenger and emissary of God in an attempt to heal a fractured world. Theirs was a cooperative effort; a consultation/liaison model of recovery and repair. And in cooperation with God, man was able to confront the forces of evil, and he was elevated to a new and ethical level of existence. As we read in Psalm 27:

When evildoers draw near to slander me,
When foes threaten – they stumble and fall.
Though armies be arrayed against me, I have no fear.
Though wars threaten, I remain steadfast in my faith.

Thus the Torah teaches that when all hope seems lost, man surrenders to numinous authority, opposes chaos, and emerges as a healthy human being.

This guide is designed to further the growth of ethical man through nurturing the mental health of all children who have been victimized by war, crisis or disease. It is a compilation of ideas, strategies and interventions that I have successfully used in my twenty-three years of working with children in pain. The theories I offer in this guide reflect the integration of many great thinkers in the disciplines of religion, philosophy and psychology. In particular, many of my psychology interventions are built upon the wisdom of trauma specialists Beverly James, PhD, and Ronnie Janoff-Bullman, PhD. The integration of religion with psychology is inspired by the writings of Rabbi Joseph Soloveitchik, who was a leading Talmudic scholar of the twentieth century. It is my hope, and prayer, that the use of this guide will help you, the reader, and the child in your care, to regain a sense of safety, connection and faith, so that together, we may all reclaim humanity.

– N.J.F.
New York, USA
9 Elul, 5775

I. Clinical Definitions of Trauma

IN ORDER TO help the child who is facing ongoing trauma, we must first understand what lies at the core of a child's internal world. Most of us hold basic views or theories about ourselves and about the world we live in. Children, too, create personal theories of their world and the people in it; and these theories guide their assumptions and expectations, allowing them to function effectively. Most children have three fundamental expectations about the world; namely that it is a benevolent place, filled with ultimate meaning and with opportunities to experience self-worth. But when an unprecedented event occurs that challenges a child's personal theory, and creates a rift in his core assumptions about the world and its people, trauma and its attendant reactions ensue. As a result, the child in pain is at risk for suffering from the following side effects:

- ◻ A sense of disempowerment
- ◻ Lack of faith in the order of the world
- ◻ Alienation and disconnection from others

And we learn that recovery requires:

- ✓ Empowering the victim or survivor of a trauma
- ✓ Re-establishing a sense of faith

✓ Creating new and healthy connections and
  attachments

**Trauma therapist Beverly James states that psycholog-
ical trauma occurs when an actual or perceived threat
of danger (most often life-threatening) overwhelms a
child's personal theory of the world, and compromises
his usual and normal coping abilities.**

The diagnosis for traumatization in children should be
based upon the *context* and the *meaning* of the experience
for the child, *not the actual event*. For example:

Getting lost in a large department store or shopping
mall can be quite benign to an adult, but very threaten-
ing to a child;

Whereas

News reports about terror factions growing in Iraq
may frighten an adult, while the child, who lacks understanding of the potential threat of danger, may feel
surprisingly safe.

**Thus, we must understand the meaning of the traumatic
event for the child.**

Unfortunately, many well-meaning adults miss the signs
or cues that children share with regard to their fears.
Scared children do not speak directly about their feelings
of fear, sadness or despair. Rather, they speak in metaphor
and poetry, through play, temper tantrums or tears. Only

when we listen closely and with a child's ear will we learn the secret, symbolic language they speak. If we are quiet, patient and loving, we will hear their heartfelt expressions of a traumatic memory or event.

Most researchers of Post Traumatic Stress Disorder believe that a child's expression of the trauma will be influenced by four factors:

1. Age of the Child and Cognitive Growth
Depending upon a child's age, trauma and all that accompanies it, takes on new and changing definitions. Thus, in listening closely to their stories, adults need to be aware of the developmental changes and attendant fears and concerns that children's cognitions undergo. When discussing the concept of death with a child, for example, age and cognitive growth must be appreciated. In particular, before the age of seven or eight, children have not yet achieved the concept that death is *irreversible* – that once a person dies, there is no returning to life; that death is *universal* – everyone dies, not just pets and old people; and that death is *caused by something* – be it illness, accident, old age, or even terrorism.

2. The Child's Behavioral Style
The most widely quoted psychology researchers define behavioral style as persistent patterns in temperament or action; namely the *how* of behavior. This is distinguished from motivation (the *why*) and content (the *what*) of behavior. A child's behavioral style may fall into one of three categories:

The **Easy Child** who is positive in mood, regular in bodily functions, adaptable and comfortable in new situations;

The **Difficult Child** who is often negative in mood, irregular in bodily functions, low in adaptability, and withdrawing rather than approaching in new situations;

The **Slow-to-Warm-Up Child** who is mild in intensity and mood, relatively regular in bodily functions, withdrawing initially from new situations, but eventually becoming more like an Easy Child as time passes.

Developing an understanding of the innate behavioral profile of the child in your care will aid in an appreciation of how he experiences, integrates and expresses his sorrow and fear.

3. The Child's Family History

Children's responses to trauma will vary according to their family history of difficult life events. Many families have suffered previous losses, either through natural events or terrorist attacks and involvement in war. Children raised in homes such as these are likely to become more vigilant and aware of the sound of sirens overhead, and understand the urgent need to enter a bomb shelter or inner stairwell or room of the house for safety. However, these same children are at greater risk for Post Traumatic Stress reactions as the traumatic events will likely stimulate or "trigger" unresolved fears from their past.

4. The Child's Social World

When adults are available, emotionally present and willing to provide honest and gentle answers to traumatized children's questions, young people's understanding of the traumatic events will be more realistic, and also less frightening. Unfortunately, many adults are exposed to, and impacted by, the same negative events that their children are, and they are often unable to separate their own fears from those of their children. Additionally, some children live in homes that are impacted by divorce, death or geographical difficulties. These are all variables that will affect a child's understanding of the trauma.

I saw this while working with a seven-year-old boy whose father was killed in the attacks on the Twin Towers in 2001. David was an only child, adopted from an Arabic country, and being raised by his Jewish parents in Brooklyn, New York. David's understanding of what happened to his father on September 11 was filtered through his bereft mother's anger and shock, and his grandmother's despair and loneliness. There were no older brothers, uncles or father figures available to help David manage his inner world; and in that first year after the trauma occurred, David was left to make sense of his loss with little guidance. However, with the primary goals of *security, faith,* and *empowerment,* trauma therapy helped David to find a healthy sense of safety, hope, and reconnection with the outside world.

II. Signs and Symptoms of Trauma in Children

RESEARCH IN PSYCHOLOGY has consistently shown that human exposure to a long-standing series of frightening events can lead to a diagnosis of Post Traumatic Stress Disorder or PTSD. The diagnosis of PTSD was originally applied to soldiers experiencing the effects of combat exposure during the Vietnam War. Today, however, the diagnosis of PTSD is applied to all persons who have been exposed to an extreme traumatic stressor, such as a life-threatening event, atrocity, or psychic or bodily assault that threatens their personal integrity, sense of safety and mortality.

PTSD and psychic trauma in children, like in many adults, take on several identifying characteristics. They are:

- **Flashbacks** – visualized or repeatedly-perceived memories of the trauma
- **Flash forwards** – involuntary fantasies of a possible funeral or repeat terror
- **Hyper-vigilance** to the recurrence of danger
- **Repetitive behaviors** – otherwise forbidden reenactments through play or bodily activity

- **The absence of a belief** in a positive or limitless future
- **Fears** of things that are specifically related to the actual event (e.g., sirens)
- **Fear of the mundane** or unrelated objects or events – the dark, strangers, food, animals, etc.
- **Changes in attitude** about the world and the people in it
- **Numbness/shock** – "I feel nothing." "That didn't happen to me."
- **Withdrawal** – removal of self from ordinary activities and attachments
- **Clinginess** – regression in which the child acts younger and more needy
- **Rage/irritability** – outbursts of anger that are often incongruous to content
- **Disruptions in memory** –wavering in certainty and detail of a past event
- **Nightmares** – the unconscious fear expressed during sleep

All of these are adaptive, albeit negative, behaviors that are employed by the child to help him avoid or survive the pain he feels. We must be vigilant to their presence and, once we have created an environment for the child that is filled with *safety and security*, we must honor, appreciate and allow the child's need for their expression.

Children grieve differently than teenagers; and both grieve differently than adults. More specifically, children grieve in spurts. They have good days and bad days; and sometimes it even looks as if their sadness has gone away completely. But eventually and seemingly out of nowhere, the child will show signs of internal struggle again. His expressions of fear and sorrow will be varied, and sometimes veiled beneath other, more "acceptable" emotions. Thus, as listed above, we may witness a child's response to trauma through temper tantrums, difficulty sleeping, changes in appetite, lack of motivation, fluctuation in mood, problems with peers, poor concentration, school difficulties, forgetfulness, eating issues, clinging behaviors, withdrawing behaviors, as well as tears.

Teens, on the other hand, respond in a different way to trauma. Some teens openly cry or speak about their feelings, while others are more comfortable emoting through poetry, late-night conversations on the internet with friends or strangers, and compulsive involvement in music or art. Many teenagers wish to spend large amounts of time alone rather than with their own family. This may be a teen's way of trying not to over-burden an already overwhelmed parent, sibling or relative.

Regardless of their age, children and teens need to discuss what life will be like now that the trauma has occurred. They need to *openly protest* the trauma that they have experienced before they can make sense of it. Some common questions I have been asked include:

What will life be like without my loved one in it?
What will our family be like when the threat of bombs is over?
When will I stop looking over my shoulder?
Why did God make such a bad world?
Can there really be a God in heaven?

Adults rarely have a good answer for these types of questions. Oftentimes, seeing a child in this type of pain is difficult for an adult to bear, and the answers they give will likely fall short of satisfying the child's needs. Thus, at times such as these, silence, a warm hug or a gentle touch can become the most helpful means of assurance and communication with a hurt child.

In the following section, we will explore more professional approaches to answering these difficult questions.

III. Treatment Approaches

A. THE POWER OF STORY

WHEN YOUR RELATIONSHIP with the child feels safe enough, (and *only* when the child feels safe) he will begin to explore the incident.

Remember the three primary goals of empowerment, faith and connection.

(a) Children need to tell their story

Every child who has experienced a trauma has a story to tell. It may be the story of the moment they heard the news that their father was killed; or the story of the day they saw a rocket explode under the Iron Dome in the sky. It may be an innocuous story of a bully who made fun of them at school; or a terrifying story of seeing blood and pain on the body of a child who was hit by a missile. Children need to tell their story, in all its gory detail, and for as long as they need to tell it.

Why?

Because **grief and trauma are like radioactive waste: They are non-biodegradable.** Traumatic memories do not go away simply because we bury them deep inside our psyches. This is a mistake many adults and child psychologists alike make all the time. Children's memories, when buried underground, will eventually fester and poison the soil of their mental and physical well-being. Moreover, their memories will find their way to consciousness through nightmares, poor sleeping patterns, peer relation problems, compromised school performance, changes in appetite, and fluctuations in weight, motivation and drive.

Remember: **If we do not cry with our eyes, we will cry with another organ in our body, or with another behavior.**

This is why we must let frightened children tell their story; and allow the free play of their imagination to lead the dialogue between patient and counselor. This is necessary trauma de-briefing. Dr. Clarissa Pinkola-Estes, an American Psychoanalyst, refers to this *telling of story* as a healing art. Estes uses storytelling, and the interpretation of fairytales and dreams, as a means of review and exploration. For her, it involves the careful re-exposure of the traumatic memories inside the child that may have otherwise been locked deep within the unconscious. She says:

> Whenever a fairytale is told, it becomes night. No matter where the dwelling, no matter the time . . . the telling of tales causes a starry sky and a white moon to creep from the eaves and hover over the heads of the listeners. . . . . The story we hear is our bounty to work with, to use toward soul-making.

In this tradition, the best stories, the deepest medicines, are considered to be written like a light tattoo on the skin of the one who has lived them. The training, [the healing,] comes from the reading of this faint writing upon the soul, from the development of what is found there. . . . Story as medicine drums itself up from the teller's bones. It comes fluttering through the dark unbidden. It is mined in the farther reaches of the psyche. It is lived, not memorized.

Although some use stories as entertainment only, they are, in their oldest sense, a healing art. Some are called to this healing art, and the best, to my lights, are those who have lain with the story and found all its matching parts inside themselves and at depth.

Thus, according to trauma therapists and child psychologists alike, it is through the recounting of fear and trauma, grief and despair, that a child eventually becomes able to unhinge it from its hidden place in the unconscious.

Five Ways That the "Telling of Story" Leads to Healing

1. Storytelling is a child's way of gaining control over the loss

Children who have been exposed to trauma are left with a sense of *disempowerment and a loss of control.* Whereas healthy children often feel invincible (they have magical thoughts of an ordered world over which they have some measure of control), traumatized children are suddenly swept into a new world, filled with doubt and uncertainty, unpredictability and the expectation of recurring danger. Their belief in justice and mercy has been challenged, and they come to learn that, sometimes, bad things happen even to good people. In the words of one adolescent patient:

> Now I know that the future belongs to no one. Now I no longer try to hold on to things that aren't mine to begin with. How I envy my friends' ability to feel in control of their own destiny.

Thus, the child's compulsive recounting of his story helps him to *own* the traumatic event. It is his way of gaining control over the crisis, of achieving mastery over what happened to him and his family. "This is *my* story" he tells himself. "And the more I tell it, the more I get used to it. And the more I get used to this new world I was thrown into, the sooner I will get better." In the words of one wise patient:

> I didn't enter into this trauma. This trauma entered into *me*, and I have to get it out of me. Telling you what happened is my way of getting it out.

An example of this compulsive repetition of story was exemplified in the family members of victims of TWA Flight 800 which exploded over the waters of Long Island, New York, in 1995. I was providing support to grieving mothers and fathers who were awaiting news of the recovery of their loved ones' bodies. Night after night I sat with these families at a hotel at John F Kennedy Airport. And night after night they would tell me the very same story of where they were when they heard the news of the plane crash; or of what their loved one must have been thinking before the explosion occurred. At first I thought that these people had forgotten what they had told me. I feared there was some sort of traumatic amnesia that took hold of the room. But after two weeks of sitting quietly and patiently listening to the families' repetition of their stories, I began to realize that it was not important whether or not I *heard* their story, it was only important that they *said* it.

Many people are hurt by life's traumas. And these families in particular had an awful story to tell. The more I listened with a compassionate and curious ear, the more I found that they began to *own* their story. They were unconsciously gaining mastery over the reality of what had happened to their loved ones, and what had happened to them as bereft survivors.

2. Storytelling helps the child accept what happened without silencing or minimizing

Well-meaning adults rarely allow children the freedom to express their despair for fear that the child will act upon his sadness. "My life as I know it has changed forever!" some hurt children cry. The adults in a child's world search for his return to a "lighter" self. They define "healing" through actions of happiness, and they naively offer affirmations of hope. But these words may actually make the child feel worse at this time. Hopeful statements include:

"Time will help you heal."
"Everything works out for the best."
"God gives and God takes.'
"God only gives you what you can handle."
"It's time to move on."

Adults want to fix what they perceive as broken in a child's world, unaware that it is not their job to fix anything.

Children who have been hurt by trauma search for peers as well as adults who understand sadness as they do. They want to cry without being judged, and laugh without being questioned. Children learn quickly who they can trust, and who they cannot. I often say that the more academic degrees you have after your name, the less a child will talk to you. In the hospital rooms of terminally ill patients where I used to work, it was the woman who cleaned the bathrooms, or the man who collected the menus for lunch, that heard the most vulnerable stories from sick children. But when a doctor would walk in, dressed in a white lab coat bearing a name tag with a full title and degree, most children would pretend to be asleep.

Thus, when we listen to a child's story of trauma, in all of its gory detail, without saying well-intentioned but naïve words of comfort and assurance, we help him to feel safe while at the same time honoring his vulnerability. And vulnerability in the context of a healthy therapeutic relationship is where the healing begins.

3. Storytelling helps the child integrate the traumatic event into memory

In the words of one patient, "my scary memories circle around the outside of my head, always searching for a place to hide." This child's statement supports findings from neurophysiology research that suggest that traumatizing events are processed differently than are normative and/or common events in the brains of young people. Whereas common daily events become blended and remain accessible to a child's awareness, traumatic events are not integrated into children's memories. Rather, they remain separate, and partially or fully out of consciousness. As a result, children who face ongoing trauma are at risk for suffering from **disruptions of memory.** Simply put, their brains are too scared or shocked to make sense of the horrors that illness, war and destruction have created in their world.

Disruptions in memory are maladaptive, albeit common childhood reactions to traumatic events. They are a child's unconscious way of surviving the pain they witnessed or endured. Memory disruptions can manifest in one of three different ways, and they are closely associated to the senses of smell and sound:

- **Flashbacks:** These are sudden and unexpected intrusive images of the horrifying event, most commonly occurring when a child least expects it. For example, listening to music on the radio, or shopping in a store where there is an odor similar to one that was around during the traumatic event, can suddenly trigger an unbidden visual memory that sets a child back days, if not weeks, in his recovery.

- **Nightmares:** These are unconscious (buried) memories of the trauma that are more freely expressed during sleep. Research in neuropsychology asserts that transmitters in the brain fire at different rates during night- as opposed to day- time hours. As a result, traumatized children who have buried their memories deep inside are at risk for re-experiencing many of them in their sleep.

- **Protective Denial** (or the *"That Never Happened to Me" Syndrome*)**:** This is a disruption in memory that is employed by the child to survive significant traumatic loss. An example of protective denial in my work occurred with two young brothers who were riding in a car with their mother, father, and two older siblings when a siren caused the car to swerve out of control and hit an oncoming bus. My two patients were the only survivors of the accident and, when asked where they were sitting in the car during the event, their answer to me was, "We were not in the car that night."

Thus, when we allow a traumatized child to tell his story of fear, and when we listen with a trained ear that resists a silencing or minimizing of the event, we help him to integrate the trauma into his memory. This is important for several reasons. First, it normalizes the child who doesn't understand why he is having so many flashbacks or nightmares. Second, it helps in the reduction of these post-traumatic responses, and places the scared child well on his way toward recovery.

4. Storytelling helps the child "place" the grief some-where where it no longer defines or assaults him
Children who have experienced a tragedy are at greater risk for defining themselves as *survivors, or victims, or sufferers* because of a horrible event. Their story of fear, if not handled carefully, can become the new and sole definition of who they are. "I am motherless, or fatherless, or brotherless" I often hear children say. "I am different because I lived for thirty days in and out of bomb shelters." While

self-expression is indeed essential for healing, children need to eventually integrate their grief into a larger and healthier sense of self. We are all more than the sum of our most frightening events; when we listen carefully to a child's story, replete with its intimations of hope and wishful thinking, we can help him to *place* his trauma somewhere inside where it no longer defines and/or assaults him. Eventually, it is the spoken word, rather than traumatic mental images, that becomes the medium through which the child processes his memory.

Researchers and psychologists who study grief and bereavement suggest that the process of helping a child "place" his grief somewhere is most successfully facilitated through performing a "ritual event." Traumatized children benefit from:

- Writing or drawing their feelings onto paper
- Writing or drawing on a balloon that they can ultimately send off to heaven
- Planting a tree
- Creating a memory box, scrapbook or photo album

Not all ritual events involve the creation of something tangible and precious. Some may actually entail the destruction of something that reminds the child of the enemy that "took my mother" or of the "missiles that ruined my summer." Some children I worked with:

- Burned a hat or shirt they wore the month they found themselves in and out of bomb shelters
- Threw away a book they read during the time the trauma occurred

- Created a treasure box out of Lego toys and then
  destroyed it in an effort to "be done with the trauma
  that kept us hostage"

Thus, helping a child to place his grief somewhere may be
symbolic, or it may be concrete and literal. For some, it
will generate a sense of relief when performed, while for
others it may, for a time, stimulate more feelings of sorrow.
Regardless of how it moves a child, however, it will eventually help him to live "alongside" his fear and sadness, and
to not live "behind it."

5. Storytelling brings the child closer to a relationship with the Ultimate Listener

The healing power of story has its roots in Jewish thought,
specifically in the power of prayer or *tefilla*. As the Rav
asserts, when man seeks God through prayer, God listens;
and when pain and distress take on a public character, God
responds to the community who prays. Similarly, Maimonides tells us that it is a commandment to "cry out and blow
the trumpets ... whenever troubles befall the community"
(Hilkhot Tefilla 1:1), and Nahmanides instructs that, in
troublesome times, there is a biblical commandment of
prayer. Moreover, throughout the Bible we see that when
man suffers from emotional constriction (tzara), he seeks
solace through prayer.

As it says in Samuel 22:7:

In my anguish I called on the Lord,
Cried out to my God;
In His abode He heard my voice,
My cry entered His ears.

Man in need "lifts his eyes towards the mountain" and is blessed. However, as we have all experienced in our lives, the blessing is not always found in the outcome of the prayer, but rather in the process of petition itself. For, as the Rav reminds us, the foundation of prayer is not in the conviction of its efficacy, but in the formation of a metaphysical fellowship through which healing and redemption can occur. More specifically, when we engage in *tefilla* (prayer), we find the ultimate Listener. Whether or not the Listener will accept our petition or plea remains unknown. But through our prayer, an intimate, majestic and healing relationship has been born. Most importantly, the power of telling our story facilitates our ability to hear and obey God's words.

(b) Exploration of a child's story must be carefully paced

In helping young people come to terms with trauma and loss, adults often confuse their own views of the event with those of the child in their care. In understanding trauma from the child's perspective, however, we need to be willing to enter the child's world. This requires us to be open-minded, curious, creative and accepting. Specifically, magical thoughts are prominent features of all children's cognitive processes. So when listening to a story of trauma, we must remember that children understand and speak a different language than we do, especially during times of stress and crisis. Children's vocabulary about loss is filled with metaphor, magic and sometimes even peril. Fantasies of angels, ghosts, villains and mythical characters pervade the internal world of the traumatized child. And what children don't say with words, they will say with their actions, such as temper tantrums, oppositional behaviors, regressive conduct, hunger, withdrawal, clinginess and tears.

Moreover, frightened children can only tolerate direct dialogue, or even symbolic play about the traumatic event, for about eight minutes before it becomes damaging to their inner peace. You will see this happening as children who are over-exposed to their own traumatic memories will regress and begin to act-out. They will change the topic, run around the room, or simply shut down and not speak. Thus, the most effective way to connect with a traumatized child is to have a **session within a session.** This is an eight minute dialogue embedded within the frame of a forty-five minute interaction. When done this way, we discover that conducting trauma therapy is quite similar to conducting a symphony. Adapted from Dr. Marshall Duke of Emory University, the formula is stated as follows:

Primary Theme

All good symphonies begin with a *primary theme*. For the traumatized child, this may be the "news of the week in review." It may involve the playing of a simple card game or board game, or engaging in a lighthearted conversation replete with laughter and good will. It may involve a bit of gossip about who is fighting with whom at school, or about a favorite song or television show that was recently heard or viewed.

Secondary Theme

Shortly after the session begins, as in a symphony, there is a *secondary theme*. For the child, this part of the dialogue is marked by tentative expressions of fear, mixed with rigid, almost robot-like speech. Memories of the traumatic event are coming to the surface, and the interaction may be filled with moments of hesitation, long pauses, or complete silence. There may be moments of little to no eye-contact, and the child's posture may reflect a need for distance (e.g., arms folded over chest, head down, or body in a fetal position).

Crescendo Phase

This is where the *primary theme* meets the *secondary theme* in our work. In a symphony, this is represented by cacophony and musical discord; sharp notes colliding with flat ones, and loud horns mixed with symbols and percussion. For the traumatized child, this part of the session is represented by temper tantrums, tears, oppositional behavior and, sometimes, direct words of shame, horror and sorrow. It is important to allow these uncomfortable expressions of fear and discord, for we, the inspired listener, are essentially saying without words:

"Go ahead. I can take it. Your pain doesn't scare or overwhelm me."

Recapitulation of the Primary Theme

In all good symphonies, no one leaves the theatre in the midst of the fireworks. Good conductors usually end the musical score with a quiet review of the theme they started with, and in some overtures, the entire movement ends on one quiet note. This is exactly how we end our dialogue with a scared or traumatized child. No one leaves the office in tears. No child walks to the edge of a symbolic cliff and stays there. After an eight minute *crescendo phase* of dialogue, we enter into a lighter phase of the interaction; perhaps a discussion of plans

for the coming weekend, or a simple game of cards that
is devoid of heavy emotion. In doing trauma work with
children (unlike working with adults), it is important to
end an interaction with a verbal gift of hope and safety.
"You came to the right place" we tell the child. "You are
brave and I am proud of you."

Why is pacing the dialogue important?
Because: it teaches the child that emotions have a begin-
ning, middle, and an end.

Traumatized children have lost the chance to play, laugh
and think positively about their future. They have become,
as Beverly James once said, anesthetized by fear. They
have shut themselves off from their emotions in an effort
to survive. As a result, many are afraid that if they cry, they
may never stop crying; or if they focus on the traumatic
event, it may never leave them. But when we create structure in our dialogue, we teach the child that it is okay, even
safe, to cry, because after crying there is laughter. Indeed,
in his famous third chapter, Kohelet (3:2-8) gave poetic
expression to the welcome continuum of our changing
emotions:

> To everything there is a season, and a time to every pur-
> pose under the heaven . . . a time to love, and a time to
> hate . . . a time to laugh and a time to cry.

Thus, just as in psychology, the Torah teaches that the
whole range of the emotional spectrum is present in each
one of our affective experiences. And, as the Rav asserts,
we must indeed know how to love and to hate; we must

appreciate the art of reaching out to others in need, while understanding the craft of resisting injustice and wrong-doing. Structure in the dialogue with a frightened child thus begins this very process.

(c) Listening to a child's story involves the "Art of Unknowing"

There is an art to **not knowing** what a child will say next. Many adults forget this, and they end up speaking for the child in need, or perhaps finishing his sentences and assuming they fully understand his point of view. This is known in psychology as **the silencing effect,** and it infers that when an adult in a traumatized child's world assumes to know what he is talking about, he runs the risk of silencing the child who has a story to tell. Children speak a different language than adults; their world is special and unique in a way that is likely to be misunderstood. Even if we think we know what a child is going to say next, it is wise to sit quietly and wait. For in waiting, we will be gifted with fuller descriptions of feelings or fears that may be stuck deep within the child's psyche.

An illustration of the **art of unknowing** is seen in the dialogue of a young boy whose sister lost her eye because of cancer. Benjamin was seven when I met him, and he was frightened about seeing the face of his little sister after she completed her surgery. He and his mother sat together in my office, and he openly asked questions about the procedure:

"What did the doctors do with her eye?" Ben asked.

"I don't know Ben," his mother answered. "I think they put it under a microscope to study it."

"When they're done looking at it, what will they do
with it?"

"I don't know Ben," she said.

"Can they give it back?"

"I don't think so," she said.

"Why not?"

"Because they may still have to look at all of the little
parts," his mother said reluctantly.

Not quite certain of where this conversation was going,
and not in complete understanding what the boy was trying to express here, I asked,

"What would you do with the eye, Ben?"

"I'd save it," he said firmly.

"Save it?!" Mom exclaimed.

"Yeah, I'd put it in a jar and leave it in my bedroom."
He cried.

"Oh Ben, that's disgusting," Mom said.

"No its not," I whispered to Ben supportively. "I think
it's beautiful. After all, your sister's eye was a part of her.
It was something you looked into every day of her life.
It's a piece of her that you can no longer see. Of course
you'd want it with you."

At this point Ben's mother began to cry. When I asked her
what her tears were saying, she answered,

"You know, this is the first time I cried about what happened. You see, after the surgery was over, the doctors
came in and congratulated me. And I said to the doctors, 'Why are you congratulating me? My little girl just

lost her eye.' And they said, 'Yes, that is true. But you're daughter is now cancer free.' And from that moment on, I never cried again. But now I am finally realizing how much we lost and how I forgot to grieve."

This story illustrates the wisdom of *not knowing* what a child is going to say or ask next. If I had assumed to know what Ben was thinking when he asked about his sister's eye, I would not have discovered the unresolved sorrow that was inside of his mother. In addition, without careful questioning, I would not have noticed Ben's compulsive need to take care of his mother at this time.

When working with children who are in the *midst* of an ongoing trauma, the questions we ask need to be even more carefully constructed. Children in the middle of a trauma speak more symbolically than with direct language. We, the listener, must work hard to discern what is actually being said with patience and creativity. An example of this type of *unknowing* is illustrated in the case of Danny, a 16-year-old boy who had a message to convey at the end of his short life. I visited Danny in the hospital as he lay dying from a rare and inoperable cancer. Quietly, I sat by his bedside and asked the following:

"How are you feeling, Buddy?"
"You have a funeral to go to?" Danny responded.
"No. What?"
"You have a funeral to go to." he repeated.
"No, Buddy." I said. "I asked you how you were feeling."
"Oh," he answered. "I thought you said you had a funeral to go to."

"No," I assured him.

Danny had a story to tell, and he had chosen me to be his listener. As I sat there, Danny held tight to an oxygen tube he needed for help with breathing and, using it like a microphone, said the following words to me:

> "I made a cake."
> "You made a cake," I repeated.
> "Yeah."
> "I didn't know you could cook."
> "Yeah," he answered.
> "Who's it for?" I asked.
> "For me."
> "What's the occasion?"
> "I don't know," he cried.
> "What's written on the cake?"
> "For Danny only," he said.
> "Just for you?"
> "Yeah."
> "What flavor is it?"
> "It's chocolate and vanilla."
> "Who can eat the cake?"
> "Nobody. Only me . . . and you."

Together, Danny and I talked in metaphor as I carefully attempted to learn the message he was trying to say to me.

> "You and me, Danny?"
> "Yeah," he replied. "Danny and Norman. But you better get there in time."
> "What's the rush?" I asked.

"It may not be there when you get there," he answered.

"Why not?"

"I may eat it all. And I don't want to eat it all," he said.

"Where's there, Danny? Where are we?"

"My house. It's in my house. I live there. I've gotta clean up a lot of things. I left a mess."

"You left a mess?"

"Yeah."

"Where?"

"In the kitchen. I've gotta clean things up. I left the stove on."

"How can I help you clean, Danny?" I asked. "Is there a way I can help?"

At that very moment, in the middle of his story, a nurse entered the room, preceded by her medicine cart.

"Time to take your vitals," she announced loudly.

"Can this wait until later?" I urged.

"Afraid not," the nurse answered.

I sat there for a minute, confused as to how to proceed. Danny had a story to tell, a message to convey, but the nurse had her job to do. I waited until the nurse finished checking his vitals, turned down the lights, and asked Danny about his cake.

"Where were we?" he asked.

"We were in the kitchen," I smiled. "You told me to hurry or I might not make it."

"Oh yeah. You're there," he answered.

"I'm there?"

"Yeah. And there's a beautiful woman. She loves me. And she finds you attractive. She likes you."

"Likes me?" I asked.

"Yes. And she wants to marry you. I give her to you. I let you have her."

"Why Danny?"

"Because she likes you and you like her. But you're not always nice to her."

"I'm not?"

"Not all the time. And she's gonna leave you."

"Leave me? What have I done wrong?"

"You never come home. You're always working. You're not home for dinner," he explained.

"How can I change things, Danny?"

"She needs you," was his reply.

"What does she need?"

"She needs you to comfort her."

In that moment, I understood what it was that Danny was trying to say to me. I understood his fears for his lonely mother, who, at the end of each tired day, waited for his father to comfort and protect her. But his father rarely came home. Danny was her only true friend. Theirs was a rare and beautiful connection. And now that he was dying, he knew his mother would need a new best friend. In engaging in this dialogue with Danny, I tried to assume a curious, interested and *almost confused* posture. And in not fully comprehending what he was trying to say to me, I was able to learn more about his fears, convey them to his parents and, hopefully, lift the guilt or worry that weighed down his spirit.

The level of compassion necessary to facilitate this

type of healing is predicated on Jewish thought. Moses Maimonides suggested this idea when he emphasized the notion of Avodah she'baLev, or "worship of the heart." According to Maimonides, moral and religious actions must always be endowed with compassion and understanding. In essence, service to fellow man can only be achieved with empathy and love.

The Gemara supports this notion as well, as it records several incidents in which sages who were afflicted with suffering required the help of another. In particular, when Rabbi Yochanan fell ill, his counterpart Rabbi Chanina went to visit him, asking:

> "Are these afflictions dear to you?"
>
> Rabbi Yochanan answered, "Neither they nor their reward."
>
> Rabbi Chanina then said to him: "Give me your hand," and Rabbi Chanina revived him.
>
> The Gemara asks, "Why did Rabbi Yochanan need another rabbi's help? Why couldn't he revive himself?"
>
> And the Gemara answers, "A captive cannot release himself from prison. He needs help from someone outside." (*Bavli Berachos* 5b)

Thus, Jewish faith teaches us that when we are experiencing a trauma, we need the strength of a compassionate other to redeem us from our darkness. Without this help, this loving attention and true understanding, we cannot be freed from our suffering and our spirit may not be healed. Thus, we follow Jewish law and attempt to help the child in our care. Through our love, we hope the child can reach outward and upward for help and support, so that he may "acquire a heart of wisdom" and discover new ways to master his pain and sorrow.

B. THE POWER OF PLAY

1. Permission

Traumatized children need to be given permission to play.

Healthy play involves the use of the senses (looking, listening, tasting, smelling and touching), as well as an appropriate use of personal space, body, and exchange of ideas. But children who have been traumatized have lost the inner security and freedom that facilitates healthy play. Many have been expected by the adults in their world to "keep a stiff upper lip"; to be stoic, strong and brave. Conversely, some traumatized children have been expected to emote and over-express their sorrows to well-meaning adults. As a result, their play becomes fragmented, and it is marked by episodes of constricted verbalizations, remoteness and self-protection.

The adults in a frightened child's world need to be reminded to perform the simple act of playing a game with them. Many students and new psychotherapists comment on how difficult this is for them, regardless of its apparent simplicity. They assume that merely playing a game for thirty minutes with a scared child is "a waste of time." They complain that there is little or no dialogue, no tears and no moment of revelation or epiphany from the child. But they forget an important fact about trauma therapy; namely, that *play is therapy.* It involves the establishment of healthy connections between adult and child, replete with the normal and safe interactions of understanding, reciprocity and respect. An illustration of this common mistake we make with children is described below.

El'ad was a seven-year-old boy with whom I worked in an absorption center in Maalot, Israel. He had witnessed his mother's murder in an ambush while escaping from Ethiopia through the Sudan. After safely being placed with relatives already living in the absorption center, El'ad was brought to my office with the hope that he would be able to express his fears about the trauma he endured. Our initial session consisted simply of playing a popular and age-appropriate board game. We laughed, played and had a nice time together. At the end of our meeting, El'ad asked if he could take a little toy home from the office. I looked around and noticed that there were many little plastic toys just like it in the room, and I figured that one less toy would not be missed. I told him to hold on to it and to remember to bring it back with him at our next meeting.

At first reflection, I told myself that I gave El'ad the figurine because it was a "transitional object" (an object that would help him to remember our nice time together). In retrospect, however, I realize that I gave El'ad the toy for a different reason entirely. I was afraid that in simply playing a game, rather than helping him achieve a deep catharsis or revelation about the loss of his mother, then I was not doing my job. But I was wrong because our play was entirely therapeutic. For in our play, there was no angry adult changing the rules on him. No one punished him when he cheated and no one teased him when he lost. In our game, a healthy adult male praised him for his persistence, laughed at his jokes, and helped him to feel important, accepted and safe. Thus I learned that by simply playing a game, I had provided a frightened little boy with one of the most effective therapy sessions of his young life.

2. Symbolic Play

The use of play with a traumatized child is also powerful because it facilitates a *symbolic language* between patient and therapist. Traumatized and frightened children rarely speak in direct language about their feelings and thoughts. Rather they speak in metaphor, through fairytale and storytelling. Sometimes they use the media of poetry, song, or imagery. And when we listen closely to the nonverbal or symbolic language that is being reflected through their play, we will discover the themes of fear, mistrust, abandonment, and anger, as well as the need for solace, safety and emotional validation.

An example of this type of symbolic play is seen through Rafi, a seven-year-old boy who spent a summer in southern Israel running with his family into and out of bomb shelters during air attacks led by Hamas militants. Rafi was over-stimulated by the sudden and unpredictable sounds of the sirens; but he was also over-exposed to information about the dangers and devastation that the bombs caused as his parents listened hourly to the news reports, all summer long.

When Rafi and I met, he quickly engaged in a game of building Lego bricks. He was intent on creating a city filled with "safes for the jewels." Together we carefully constructed safe after safe; and inside each safe we placed pretend jewels that could be protected in the event of a robbery. Rafi had a compulsive need to repeat this game week after week in my office; whenever I tried to assure him the safes would protect the jewels, Rafi found another way to show me how precarious the jewels really were. At our third meeting, Rafi mispronounced the word "jewels" in our game and instead called them "Jews." He was compulsively guiding me to keep the Jews safe in treasure boxes throughout his Lego city. While Rafi was too scared to use words to describe what he had experienced and feared, he told me through metaphor and a slip of the tongue what it was that he needed from me.

This type of play therapy can be effective with trauma victims, but it is only half of our work. If we only allow a frightened child to repeat the themes of despair and destruction every time we play with him, he may find himself overwhelmed and "stuck" in his own negative ideations. Thus, when the relationship feels safe and secure enough, we can gently move to a new level of play, namely ***reparative play.***

3. Reparative Play

This type of play introduces the themes of repair and resolution into the child's thematic world. It is not helpful to *push* a frightened child into this phase of play, but it is indeed an ultimate goal of our work with him. When the compulsive reenactment of negative themes seems to overwhelm the child, and when we don't feel that any theme of "resolution" is in sight, we may wish to integrate the ideas of "safety" or "positivity" into the game. In the case of Rafi and his need to keep "the Jews in a safe place," I introduced the reparative themes of courage, success throughout history, and God. In my fourth meeting with Rafi, for example, I created a new Lego character that was well-trained in getting robbers into jail. Together Rafi and I discussed his strengths, his long history of "cleaning up the streets," and even some supernatural powers. I allowed Rafi to create the new character's powers and abilities, and I gently nurtured any themes of safety and security that his play reflected. In time, the compulsive need to build safes disappeared and Rafi was able to use words to describe how he felt as a Jew living in a dangerous part of the world.

There are several other creative uses of play with traumatized children. Some are listed below.

4. Sessions for Soothing

Some trauma therapists suggest that a parent (or grandparent) engage in play with a frightened child in the therapy office. The family members lower the lights, soften their speech, and create a soothing ritual that helps the traumatized child to feel calm and safe. This might take the form of singing a lullaby, telling a fairytale, or simply helping the child to feel comfortable while being held by a loving other.

5. Prop Therapy

This technique involves the use of props to facilitate the child's ability to express his feelings. Props often assist in releasing a child's memory, as they provide concrete cues for retrieval and recall of a scary event.

6. Texture Therapy

Children who have been numbed by grief have lost the luxury of trusting and/or using their senses when interacting with their world. Thus, providing the child with objects of varying texture and weight can help him to locate and identify his feelings, as well as reawaken his sensory world. Cotton balls, sand paper, smooth rocks, action figures made of heavy plastic versus paper-thin dolls, all serve as agents of a child's lost voice and emotions.

7. Nature Walks

Neurophysiology research reveals that re-connecting with the elements of nature can effectively engage endorphins, dopamine and serotonin in the brain. These are natural neurotransmitters that help reduce stress, increase tolerance and activate energy in frightened people. Thus, taking a walk through a park, playing a game outside in the warm air, helping the child notice the sun on the back of his neck, or feeling the wind in his hair on a brisk cold day can help reawaken a child's sense of the world around him.

8. Humor and Cognitive Reframing

Humor has become a popular component of current psychological treatment for emotional stress. It aids in the reduction of tension, and it allows the therapist and child to create a reinterpretation or a "reframe" of the traumatic situation. Through jokes, the frightened child can express feelings that might have otherwise been too hard to share in a serious tone. An example of this positive effect follows:

While running a poetry group for children who were grieving the loss of a sibling, the children were asked to write a poem with the title, *My Question to God*. Every child wrote his or her poem in a serious tone, and everyone in the room listened with respect and appreciation as they were read out loud. Suddenly, Noa, a ten year old girl who lost her brother to cancer, stood up and read her poem proudly:

My Question to God may sound silly,
But here I go . . .
You are always over us.
Do you use the toilet bowl?"

After reading her poem, the children responded with a lightness that was both therapeutic and necessary. The mood in the group had lifted, which one boy interpreted by saying:

"Things can't be all that bad if we still remember how to laugh."

C. THE POWER OF EDUCATION

Direct and indirect teaching to the child who is traumatized is empowering. At a time when he and his family feel as if they have little or no control over the safety and well being of their loved ones, education regarding what is happening in the world around them, as well as what they can expect in the way of emotions inside of them, can be highly therapeutic as well as soothing.

1. State the facts simply

Children who are scared need to be given important information in easy and accessible words. I often tell my students to "state the facts simply, and elementarily." This is because magical thoughts pervade children's cognitive world, and their vocabulary is sometimes filled with metaphor, magic and peril. In addition, children have a concrete or literal understanding of the world around them. Thus when describing something negative that happened to a loved one, we must appreciate the cognitive limitations of the child in our care.

For example, when talking about death to a child, it is wise to say that the person's body "stopped working." We say that he "no longer burps, or hiccups, or coughs." We assure him that a loved one who has died no longer feels pain and is not sad or lonely. We speak in a language that helps him to understand that death involves the cessation of bodily functions as well as human emotions. We educate him about the rituals surrounding death so that he can feel prepared as well as empowered in the days ahead. Regardless of the child's age and cognitive awareness, honest and open discussions will yield valuable insights into his emotional needs.

2. Name emotions

Education involves naming emotions for little children who have become numb or even mute from fear. When a child cries we explain to him that he is crying because he is scared; or he is throwing things because he is angry. All too often the opposite occurs. When many adults see a child cry, they are prone to ask, "Why are you crying?" But as discussed earlier, traumatized children have lost the luxury of expressing honest emotions and they may find questions such as this one challenging, stress-inducing and impossible to answer.

3. Empower parents

From the moment a child is born, parents make a promise to protect and care for their child's every need. But when a tragedy occurs, parents may feel as if they have broken that promise. Educating parents about the complex emotional needs of their hurt or scared child gives them a sense of power. In addition, it allows the therapist to partner with the parent in an effort to effect healthy change in the child's inner life.

D. THE POWER OF CREATIVITY

There are many creative ways to help traumatized children regain a sense of safety and security, and hence, reclaim humanity. These techniques are less about therapy than they are about the expression of loss and fear through artistic effort.

1. Poetry

The use of poetry with traumatized children is not only a safe and effective means of self-expression, but the sources of inspiration are often immediate and mature, as they come from places of fear, confusion, alienation and, ultimately, hope. Some children write large, generous poems that describe their experiences in clear and succinct terms. Others write through a veil of safety, using symbolism and metaphor to describe what they feel. Regardless of what a child writes, when using this technique, we will likely find ourselves learning new and important things about the inner world of the frightened child.

When meeting with children in the south of Israel during a military operation, I shared with them a poem that was written by a pediatric oncology patient of mine who had survived cancer twenty years ago. After reading my patient's hopeful poem entitled *Me Then and Now*, an Israeli girl approached me with her own version of that poem, and it described her feelings in both literal and symbolic detail:

> **Dancing in Stairwells**
> I used to go to camp, but now I can't.
> I used to be afraid of sirens.

But now I'm used to them.
I used to think that if Hamas attacked, I would die.
But now I believe that many survive.
I used to want to be an artist.
But now I want to be a soldier.
I used to be afraid of soldiers.
But now I know they are your friends.
I used to be able to run and dance outside.
But now I dance in stairwells.
I used to think that things were hard.
But now I think that, if I can survive Hamas,
I can do anything.

M. age 10

In addition, when working with a group of children that suffered significant trauma, with the help of Scott Fried, an international health educator and author of *If I Grow Up: Talking to Teens about AIDS, Love and Staying Alive*, I asked the children to write poems about their experiences. The instructions we gave were for them to be honest and open with their thoughts. The following is what they came up with:

If I Could Ask God One Question

If I could ask God one question
It would be for Him to let my sister walk.
I would ask him this because I want her to be able to walk and because she was hurt by an explosion and she may not be able to.

D. age 11

I Am a Hero
I am a hero because I spent 45 days in the hospital with
an IV.   A. age 7

My Life Wish
My life wish is a weather report.
I wish for sunshine in my stomach.
For all my tears to help me grow.
May the wind blow all doubt and confusion out of my
head.
I wish that my cloudy days of sadness always be followed
by blue skies and confidence.
I wish for happiness, harmony, and no humidity.
                                    N. age 14

When working with children in the Pediatric Oncology
Center at a hospital in New York, I asked Vanessa Shapiro,
a teenager who survived cancer, to describe her emotional
response to her medical treatment. This is what she wrote:

Regarding chemotherapy
You told my mother once
To stop thinking of you like a curse
And more like a friend.
I think of you as both.
You are a necessary action.
A weapon in the fight against myself
You whispered once
That pain is a signal: A distraction.
That everything,
Not just you,
Had a formula

You were the monster under my bed.
But the gunman was under the covers
I did not choose you. I chose life.
I welcomed you. Of course I did.
You hated me. Of course you did.
You were a vulture and you were hungry
But you only took that which was dead
And you left the way you came.
Your job was to wait outside.
My job was to open the door.
I will never stop hating you.
I will never stop thanking you.
And I will never stop trying
to gain back my own trust.
I don't miss you.
But I'm glad we met.

2. Bumper Stickers

This is a technique that I learned from Dr. Peter Steinglass at the Ackerman Institute for Family Therapy in New York. It is a creative way of helping a traumatized child to encapsulate how he feels in only a few short words. I ask the child to imagine that he is driving in a car that has a bumper sticker on the back. On the sticker is a motto or phrase that best describes what it feels like to be in his situation. Below are a few bumper sticker mottos that children under Hamas attack in southern Israel wrote:

Live and Help Live	**It's Not Fair**
Don't Be Scared	**Miracles Happen!**
If You have a Chance, Use it	**Shit Happens!**

After each child has had the chance to write his motto and explain what it means to the group, I ask all children in the group to vote on the one that best fits the mood and experience of the collective whole. This not only offers each child a chance to express his feelings in a succinct but honest manner, but it also helps each child identify with others who feel the same way he does.

IV. Resolution of Trauma

A. THE POWER OF RELATIONSHIP

As WAS DISCUSSED earlier in this manual, the experiences of psychological trauma for children include a sense of disempowerment, a lack of faith in the order of the world, as well as a sense of alienation or disconnection from others. Although resolution of child trauma necessarily entails arduous and sometimes creative processes, the need for the establishment of a connection with a healthy other cannot be overstated. More specifically, the love and support received from other people, particularly therapists, rabbis, teachers and counselors, play a vital role in the frightened child's ability to reconstruct his inner world.

A healthy connection with a caring adult provides the hurt child with the experience of acceptance and understanding in the face of existentially challenging events. In the context of a caring relationship, the child's trauma is acknowledged, honored and put in a place where it no longer assaults the peace of his inner world. Ultimately, successful coping involves integrating the trauma into a developing sense of identity that is highlighted by benevolence, meaning and self-worth. The self needs to be rebuilt, and this involves the parallel tasks of remembering and processing the traumatic events along with the establishment of a loving and safe relationship. This relationship becomes the archetype, or roadmap, for future healthy interactions with a caring world.

An example of the rebuilding of self within a loving relationship is illustrated in the case of Matthew, a 13-year-old boy whose adoptive father had gone off to war and never returned. His adoptive mother abandoned him shortly after that, leaving Matthew in foster care, and with no information about his father's death in battle. When I met Matthew, he was angry, insolent and unwilling to connect with me. He made no eye contact, and said nothing throughout the hour we had together. This was not unexpected, as I knew that relationship building would be a frightening task for a child who had already lost so much. With most traumatized children, the creation of new connections usually begins with a regression to more infantile, remote or resistant behaviors, and this was no different in the case of Matthew and I. He sat with headphones on his ears, listened to music, and busied himself writing a story in his journal.

I decided to implement a paradoxical intervention as I knew that I had no chance of making Matthew talk to me. I leaned over, asked him if he would remove his earphones and listen to me complain for a while. I begged him not to say a single word, for I was feeling "burnt out from listening to other people's problems all day." I confided that I was "in the mood to have someone listen to *me* for a change." Matthew acquiesced and, as he pretended to be looking through stories in his journal, I offered him innocuous disclosures about my day. I talked about the strangers

I met that annoyed me, the traffic patterns that made me late for work, etc. I was performing an intervention known in Post-Modern Psychotherapy as **consulting with the expert.** Turning Matthew into the expert on "hard times" allowed him to feel confident, wise and needed.

Noticing that Matthew liked to write, I told him about my efforts to write a book of short stories and about the rejection letters I had been collecting from publishers. I suggested that he spend the rest of our session writing a story in his journal, and that I would write one as well. He agreed, and this is what he wrote:

Animal Thoughts

My name is Shai. I am a dog. I know it won't amaze many people to read something written by an animal since you've seen it done numerous times, but I'll write it anyway. When I was a pup, I was bought for the measly sum of one dollar from some people who owned my mother. I was born by a single man who lived in a mid 1800's house from his grandparents. The man walked me every day and fed me very well. It seemed I was his only friend. It went this way for many years. I put up with his job (it was very demanding,) and he put up with my antics. We were happy together and always had fun. My life was fine until the morning he went away. My life went downhill after that. A lady in the village brought me to her house. She fed me canned food instead of table scraps, and she had the nerve to cuddle me and call me her "little pooch."

My life was miserable. I became depressed. I have planned the run for weeks. I will leave when she goes to sleep and never come back. I will probably go to the woods and live like a real dog. I wonder if he misses me. He probably doesn't give me a second thought. Oh well! I guess he can get along without me. But I wonder if I can get along without him.

Matthew's story was filled with the cues I needed to understand his feelings of loss, abandonment and despair. It had the wishful features of a family history (a mid 1800's house) and memory of nurturance (We were very happy together and always had fun.) From these elements I was able to glean that Matthew was a boy who was capable of intimacy and in search of guidance. At our second meeting, I suggested that we continue writing his story together, and he was happy to oblige. He took a seat in a chair by my desk and, with his feet comfortably resting on the edge and his arms outstretched behind his head, he dictated to me the following:

> The fugitive is on the loose. He has run, and now is the time for his rebirth into society. Picture this; a large brown dog, seemingly uncivilized, shivering in a pile of rubbish in a dark alley at night. Now . . . a relatively respectable vagabond happens upon this dog and takes pity on him. He has something left of a discarded humus and pita sandwich and, going to the dog, he shares his only morsel. The man and the dog take an immediate liking to each other. They both are reminded by the other of someone in their past. The dog decides that this will be his new friend.

I added (and said out loud) the following:

> The friend feels really good about this.

At this point, the session was almost over, and Matthew was struggling to find a sentence with which to end this first chapter of our story. I sat in silence for a while, and suddenly, his reply came:

Their partnership had begun.

And at once I knew that a new and healthy relationship, where the themes of a benevolent world filled with meaning and self-worth, could begin to grow.

The relationship between counselor and patient, rabbi and congregant, teacher and student, or caretaker and child is where the growth from trauma gains its greatest momentum. We have seen how strategy, cognitive processes, creativity and ethical wisdom can begin the transformation from fear and dread in a child into expressions of hope, courage, and self awareness. But as existential psychologist Irvin Yalom once inferred, it is the relationship between caretaker and child that quietly germinates beneath everything they do together that provides the greatest healing.

Conclusion

HUMANITY, WHEN SEEN through the eyes of a traumatized child, is all too often at risk of being compromised, if
not irrevocably torn. The problem of evil has been a force
for reckoning since the beginning of time and, as generations ensue, redemption seems even harder to achieve. But
Judaism believes in the optimistic view that man can unify
the torn dimensions of humanity through the creation of
moral and ethical connections. The establishment of a
patient-counselor relationship, for example, is essential
in the healing process of the frightened child, as well as
in the repairing of a fractured world. The self, once victimized by the chaos of life, now has the opportunity to
be rebuilt within the context of a loving, accepting and
ethical bond. Moreover, this bond serves as an inspiration,
as well as a template, for other healthy interactions in the
larger world that continues to need rebuilding and repair.
Through the healing connection, the traumatized child has
been allowed to experience the necessary but terrifying
feelings of vulnerability and despair. And within this safe
bond, he has redefined himself with the qualities of valor
and courage. Many counselors try to reach the scared

child; some stand with them at the edge of the abyss and, together, look toward the frightening land that lies ahead. The best therapists, however, go the extra mile; for they know how to lovingly usher the child *into* the Promised Land, and together, they discover benevolence, meaning and self-worth along the way. And when the healer's job is done, he knows to back away gently, and respectfully, allowing the child to once again take his place in the world in which he was meant to live.

The connection which facilitates this sublimation of fear into successful functioning has its roots in the most powerful of all healing bonds; that of the covenant between man and God. The Torah refers to this connection as *"devekut"* or "cleaving." *Devekut* is an embrace of love and friendship between man and God that is free of fear and awe. The Rav describes this connection as a state of being that unites our thoughts, actions and will, allowing us to have deeper compassion and devotion to others around us. Through *devekut*, we see God in ourselves, and we are not afraid. This revelation and connection with God ultimately serves to elevate our soul. It teaches us that we are part of a grander fabric, and that our deeds, no matter how small or incomplete, heal us as well as those around us.

Thus we see how the inner world of the traumatized child can begin to be healed. Through directed action, cognitive processing, and creative methods of expression and hope, the frightened child starts on his journey toward healthier functioning. And with a sense of power, faith and attachment to a healthy love, a divine power, or the covenant itself, the growth of the child's ethical instinct is nurtured. This is not a simple task for any counselor, rabbi or well-meaning friend. But it is a goal to which we, as fellow humans, all need to aspire. For when the service of the heart is present in all that we do, the inner world of the hurt child, and the humanity of the world at large, can eventually be reclaimed.